6

A Look at

Mars

A Look at Mars

Ray Spangenburg and Kit Moser

Franklin Watts

A DIVISION OF GROLIER PUBLISHING
NEW YORK • LONDON • HONG KONG • SYDNEY
DANBURY, CONNECTICUT

In memory of
CARL SAGAN
(1934–1996), who inspired us all

Photographs ©: Art Resource, NY: 16 (Erich Lessing); Bridgeman Art Library International Ltd., London/New York: 19 (British Library), 21 (by Anonymous, Private Collection); Corbis-Bettmann: 26, 27 (Tom Bean), 31 (UPI), 17, 18; Courtesy of Jack Farmer: 73; Finley-Holiday Films: 61, 67; Lowell Observatory Photograph: 28, 100; NASA: 10, 35, 37, 40, 41, 45, 46 (JPL), 39 (LPI), 2, 59, 103 (U.S. Geological Survey, Flagstaff, Arizona), 54, 55 left, 74, 78, 84; Photo Researchers: 52, 53 (John Foster/Science Source) 69, 75 (NASA/SPL), 14 (Rev. Ronald Royer), cover (SPL), 22, 55 right, 57, 64, 92,104 (U.S. Geological Survey/SPL), 82, 83 (Detlev Van Ravenswaay/SPL); Photri: 62; The Art Archive: 25; William Hartmann: 32, 96.

Library of Congress Cataloging-in-Publication Data

Spangenburg, Ray.
    A look at Mars / by Ray Spangenburg and Kit Moser.
        p.   cm.—(Out of this world)
    Includes bibliographical references and index.
    Summary: Discusses the history of human ideas about Mars, its geology and moons, missions to the red planet, and the possibility of life on Mars.
    ISBN 0-531-11717-0 (lib. bdg.)   0-531-16513-2 (pbk.)
    1. Mars (Planet) Juvenile literature. [1. Mars (Planet)] I. Moser, Diane, 1944–
II. Title. III. Series: Out of this world (Franklin Watts, inc.)
QB641.5.S67   2000
523.43—dc21   99-37378

© 2000 Ray Spangenburg and Kit Moser
All rights reserved. Published simultaneously in Canada.
Printed in the United States of America.
1 2 3 4 5 6 7 8 9 10 R 09 08 07 06 05 04 03 02 01 00

Acknowledgments

A book like this one is the product of many minds and many conversations. The knowledge, expertise, and resources of many people flow into the mix, and we would especially like to thank those who have contributed to *A Look at Mars*.

First of all, a special appreciation to Sam Storch, Lecturer at the American Museum-Hayden Planetarium, who reviewed the manuscript and made many excellent suggestions. Also a special thanks goes to our editor at Franklin Watts, Melissa Stewart, whose steady flow of enthusiasm, creativity, energy, and clippings of late-breaking news have infused this series.

For stimulating conversations on the subject of Mars, many thanks to Christopher P. McKay, exobiologist and planetary scientist at the National Aeronautics and Space Administration (NASA) Ames Research Center (ARC); Harold P. Klein of the SETI Institute, formerly of NASA ARC, who led the Viking biology experiments; Michael Carr, geologist at the U.S. Geological Survey; and planetologist William K. Hartmann.

Finally, to Tony Reichhardt and John Rhea, once our editors at the old *Space World Magazine*, thanks for starting us out on the fascinating journey we have taken during our years of writing about space.

Contents

A Journey to Mars

More than 48 million miles (77 million kilometers) from Earth, a little robot rover about 12 inches (30 centimeters) high and as long as a skateboard crawled across the rocky surface of the desolate planet. It rolled very slowly on its six wheels, traveling only about $\frac{1}{4}$ inch (6 millimeters) per second.

Although the rover was loaded down with communications gear, scientific equipment, and cameras, its Earth-weight was only 25 pounds (11.3 kilograms). The rover's tiny computer allowed it to make some decisions on its own. The rest of its movements were ordered by scientists on Earth and relayed by way of the rover's home base—a lander craft named *Pathfinder*.

Mars *Pathfinder* (left) and its rover *Sojourner* (right) explored the surface of Mars in 1997.

The lander had cradled the little rover as they dropped together from space to the planet's surface. The lander was immobile, but its cameras and scientific equipment scanned the planet and sent pictures and information back to Earth. Its instruments also allowed scientists to watch the little six-wheeled vehicle as it ventured off on its own.

Scientists weren't the only ones tracking the little rover as it moved across the planet. Millions of people on Earth watched television coverage and read newspaper reports for news of the little rover named *Sojourner*. During the first 30 days of *Pathfinder*'s visit, computer users around the world made more than 566 million connections to the Internet site that carried news and information about the little machine's activities.

Sojourner never moved very far from the lander. It always stayed within communications range of its home base. But it had traveled more than 309 million miles (497 million km) to perform its duties. Its mission was to crawl slowly across the strange planet's face and take pictures and perform scientific tests on the planet's rocks. It wasn't an easy job. Sometimes the little machine faltered as it moved from one rock to another, but most of the time it performed remarkably well. When the little rover finished its job and stopped transmitting signals, many people on Earth felt a twinge of sadness.

For a brief period in 1997, *Sojourner* had provided Earthlings with a bird's-eye view of the mysterious planet we call Mars. By the end of the Pathfinder Mission, scientists had learned a great deal about the red planet. But for each question the mission answered, many more remain. Was there ever water on Mars? Is some water still hidden in the planet's soil? Did Mars ever support life? If so, what became of it?

Many scientists now believe that this cold and lonely place was once much more like Earth than it is today. If so, how and why did Mars change? Will Earth change in similar ways someday? Could our planet become a barren, "Mars-like" place in the future?

Sojourner and *Pathfinder* provided us with many clues, but we still seek final answers. Other missions to Mars have also contributed to our body of knowledge. No doubt, future spacecraft will teach us even more about the red planet.

In fact, as we write this book, a mission called the Mars Global Surveyor is sending scientists images and information. By the time you read it, other spacecraft to Mars may have have begun their own exciting explorations.

Our fascination with Mars will never cease, even if—and this is a big "if"—we succeed in unraveling all the planet's amazing mysteries. Earth and Mars will be forever bound together in the human mind and imagination.

Chapter 1

Early Ideas About the Universe

Long ago, people didn't have television, video games, the Internet, or the movies. None of these things had been invented yet. So when the Sun went down, humans spent a lot of time watching the night sky. Ancient peoples developed many ideas to explain the glowing points of light that lit up the darkness.

The ancient Babylonians and Greeks thought of the night sky as a canopy or dome, pierced or dotted by points of light they called stars. These people noticed that most of the lights in the celestial canopy seemed to move from east to west. A few lights, however, seemed to move restlessly in different patterns against the background of stars.

Four of these wandering points of light were white. The fifth one was especially intriguing because it had a reddish tinge.

The ancient Greeks called these five points of light *planetes*, which means "wanderers." Today, we know these five planets by the names Mercury, Venus, Jupiter, Saturn, and Mars. The Greeks also noticed that the mysterious red planet cut strange paths across the sky, moving east to west and then, for a period, seeming to move backward, retracing its path.

From earliest times, the planets and the stars played important roles in our view of the Universe and our place in it. Many people believed that the stars and planets influenced their lives. They used the night sky to develop star charts for navigation and calendars that told them when to plant their crops and when to harvest them. Other people took their beliefs too far. The results included superstitions, astrology, and even human sacrifice.

Eventually, philosophers and thinkers began to develop theories to try to explain humanity's place under the canopy of the night sky.

The Center of the Universe

Early Greek thinkers reasoned that all the planets must move in perfect, harmonious circles around Earth. The idea of harmony was basic to ancient Greek philosophy, and the great Greek philosopher Aristotle (384–322 B.C.) was a strong proponent of the Earth-centered Universe. This view of Earth and the heavens seemed logical. After all, why shouldn't everything revolve around our world?

By the second century of the Christian era, even the leaders of the Roman Catholic Church had put their stamp of approval on the idea that the Universe is geocentric, or Earth-centered. Not everyone was completely convinced by this theory, however. Some astronomers noticed imperfections in the planet's orbits. It began to look as if some planetary orbits may not be perfect circles. But people were reluctant to let go of the theory.

Around the year 140, an astronomer named Claudius Ptolemaeus, also known as Ptolemy, tried to account for the orbital imperfections. Ptolemy lived in Alexandria, Egypt, the intellectual capital of the world at that time. Ptolemy made some clever adjustments to the theory of the planets' orbits that seemed to make the whole system work. The system was very complex and awkward, but it appeared to explain the imperfections without abandoning the idea that all the planets

Around the year 140, Ptolemy reinforced a prevalent idea that Earth was at the center of the Universe. (Portrait painted around 1475 by an Italian artist.)

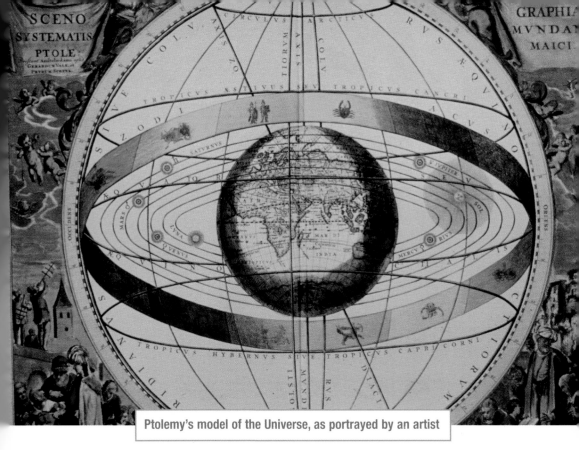

Ptolemy's model of the Universe, as portrayed by an artist

orbit Earth in perfect circles. Ptolemy's brilliant adjustments brought renewed support to the sagging theory.

As we now know, the geocentric theory of the Universe was completely wrong. Nevertheless, few people questioned it at the time—the power of the human ego was just too great, and the ideals of beauty, perfection, and harmony were too appealing. The added support of the powerful Catholic Church bolstered belief in the Earth-centered Universe. Few people dared to oppose the edicts of religious authorities.

Ptolemy's "fix" went unchallenged for more than 1,400 years. Then, in 1543, a Polish scholar named Nicolaus Copernicus (1473–1543) published *On the Revolution of the Heavenly Spheres*. The book contained a new theory about the order of the Universe. It was based on many years of carefully observing and recording the movements of the stars and planets. Copernicus suggested that Earth and all the other planets revolve in perfect circles around the Sun.

Copernicus's ideas were shocking, but most Europeans never heard of Copernicus, much less his theory. Copernicus died soon after his book was published. The pope later condemned his work, and it was placed on a list of forbidden books.

One man who did study Copernicus's work was a German mathematician named Johannes Kepler (1571–1630). Kepler was an advocate of the Copernican system, but he recognized that

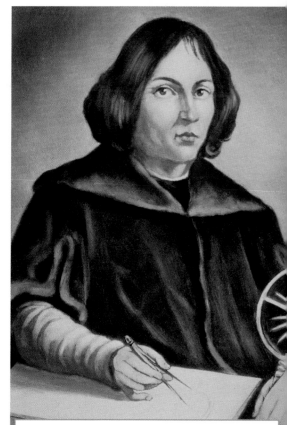

Nicolaus Copernicus calculated that the Sun, not Earth, is at the center of the solar system.

Copernicus's ideas had some flaws. Copernicus had correctly theorized that the planets orbit the Sun, but he also insisted that planets orbit in perfect circles. Today, we know that planets orbit in elongated circles, or ovals, called *ellipses*. This discovery was made by Kepler.

In 1600, Kepler began to work for a Danish astronomer named Tycho Brahe in a new observatory in Prague, Czech Republic. Using Brahe's equipment, Kepler hoped to revise Copernicus's theory into a usable model.

The model of the Universe proposed by Copernicus showed Earth and the other planets revolving around the Sun.

To do this, Kepler shifted his perspective. Instead of thinking from the point of view of Earth, he imagined himself on Mars watching Earth. He also imagined watching Mars from the Sun. By looking at the planets from different points of view, he began to realize that they have elliptical orbits. Unlike a circle, which has one center, an ellipse has two focal points. For each planet, the Sun resides at one of the orbital focal points.

More Sun-Centered Evidence

Soon, more evidence began to pile up in support of Copernicus's ideas. In the early 1600s, the great Italian astronomer Galileo Galilei (1564–1642) was among the first to look at Mars through a telescope. He noticed that the *diameter* of Mars seemed different in size, depending upon when he observed it. He made the same observation about Venus.

Galileo recognized that these differences would only occur if some parts of the orbital paths of Mars and Venus were closer to Earth than other parts. This would be impossible if the planets orbit Earth in perfect circles, but it is exactly what would happen if the planets revolve around the Sun in *elliptical orbits*. At some points in the planets' orbits, they would be on the other side of the Sun—far from Earth. Galileo realized that Copernicus had been right.

Galileo communicated these ideas widely, writing and teaching what he had learned. The Catholic Church, however, still insisted that the planets, the Sun, and the Moon all revolve around Earth. The Church forbade Galileo to teach his ideas, but Galileo couldn't stop writing and talking about what he saw to be true. In 1633, the Church put him on trial. He was found guilty of *heresy* and sentenced to house arrest for the rest of his life.

Thanks to Copernicus, Kepler, and Galileo, however, people were beginning to rethink their view of the Universe. By the middle of the seventeenth century, most of the world's major astronomers accepted that the Sun is at the center of our solar system. They understood that Earth moves in the same way as the other planets. As telescopes became more widely available, people could see the planets as disks, not just as dots of light in the sky. For the first time, people began to think of planets as "worlds." Then they began to wonder how similar these worlds were to our own planet.

This painting depicts Galileo on trial by Church authorities.

Studying the Red Planet

Meanwhile, Italian-French astronomer Giovanni Domenico Cassini (1625–1712) devoted much of his time to studying Mars. He measured the length of time the red planet takes to rotate, or make a complete turn on its axis. Mars rotates once every 24 hours and 37 minutes, so a day on Mars is just a little longer than a day on Earth.

Cassini's greatest contribution, however, came in 1672. Working with another astronomer named Jean Richer, Cassini coordinated observations of Mars simultaneously in two parts of the world. Richer observed Mars from Cayenne, French Guiana, while Cassini observed Mars from Paris, France.

The results allowed the scientists to calculate the distance from Earth to Mars. Relative distances between objects in the solar system had been known for years—since the time of Kepler. Now that the astronomers had an actual measurement for one distance, they could calculate the dimensions of the entire solar system. Previous estimates

Mars at a Glance

Mars is about 4,220 miles (6,792 km) across. Earth is almost twice as large. Mars has only about one-tenth of Earth's *mass* and one-third of its *gravity*. It is the fourth rock from the Sun, located about 141.6 million miles (227.9 million km) from the center of our solar system. The entire surface area of the red planet is about the same size as the land surfaces of Earth that are not covered by water.

Like Earth, Mars is tilted on its *axis*. This tilt causes seasons. A Martian-year is nearly twice as long as an Earth-year, so each season lasts longer on the red planet. Because Mars's orbit is very eccentric, its south pole has warmer summers than its north pole, and the planet's seasons vary in length.

During the winter, the temperature at the Martian poles drops so low that carbon dioxide condenses out of the *atmosphere* and forms a white cap. These seasonal caps sometimes extend almost halfway to the Martian equator and are visible through backyard telescopes on Earth.

No region of Mars lies beneath ocean waters or liquid lakes. However, frozen water is present at both poles, and some scientists believe frozen water may also exist elsewhere on the planet.

Both Martian poles are covered with white polar caps—composed primarily of water at the north pole and primarily of carbon dioxide at the south pole.

Mars is named for the Roman god of war. The planet has two moons, named Phobos and Deimos after the dogs of the Roman god. These moons are dark, potato-shaped chunks of rock with many *craters*. Some scientists believe they may have once been asteroids that were pulled toward Mars by the planet's gravity.

Mars

Vital Statistics

POSITION	Fourth planet from the Sun
AVERAGE DISTANCE FROM THE SUN	141.6 million miles (227.9 million km)
DIAMETER AT THE EQUATOR	4,220 miles (6,792 km) (About half of Earth's)
MASS	About one-tenth of Earth's
GRAVITY	One-third Earth's
PERIOD OF ROTATION (LENGTH OF ONE DAY)	24.6 Earth-hours
PERIOD OF REVOLUTION (LENGTH OF ONE YEAR)	686.98 Earth-days (1.88 Earth-years)
MOONS	Two

of the distance from Earth to the Sun ranged from 5 million to 40 million miles (8 to 64 million km). Cassini and Richer found that the Sun is actually 93 million miles (149.7 million km) from Earth!

Meanwhile, the Dutch astronomer and physicist Christiaan Huygens (1629–1695) found a way to improve telescope lenses. Using these superior lenses in a 23-foot (7-m) telescope, Huygens became the first person to observe markings on the surface of Mars. Nearly two centuries later, in 1830, a German banker named Wilhelm Beer (1797–1850) built his own observatory and began mapping Mars. He was the first to notice dark and bright areas on the planet's surface. Interestingly, his work included no mention of canals or waterways on the surface of the red planet. It would take another half-century for that interpretation to capture our imaginations and raise questions about life on Mars.

Chapter 2

Mars and the Imagination

By the end of the 1800s, telescopes were much more powerful, but the surface of Mars was still too far away to see clearly. While gazing through his telescope at this rusty-red blur in 1877, an Italian astronomer named Giovanni Schiaparelli noticed a series of long, thin, straight structures. He called them *canali*, an Italian word meaning "channels." Other astronomers looked for these structures, but many of them couldn't see what he was talking about. Still, his maps seemed very persuasive.

American astronomer Percival Lowell (1855–1916) took up the cause, enthusiastically combining imagination and observation. Lowell interpreted Schiaparelli's term *canali* to mean "canals." Since canals

Giovanni Schiaparelli reported that he saw *canali* or "channels" on Mars.

on Earth are artificial structures built by humans, Lowell reasoned that some form of intelligent life must have created the Martian canals.

Canals: Now You See Them, Now You Don't

Percival Lowell came from a famous Massachusetts family. His non-conformist sister Amy is still widely recognized for her poetry, and his brother Abbott served as president of Harvard University. As a boy of 15, Percival set up his first telescope beneath the roof of his family's home in Brookline. After graduating from Harvard, though, he spent most of his early adulthood traveling in such faraway places as Syria, Serbia, Turkey, Korea, and Japan. He became well known in the United States for his intriguing descriptions of those exotic places.

By the time he reached his late 30s, Lowell became fascinated by reports about the structures Schiaparelli had seen on the surface of Mars. What could these structures be? Could there be a civilization of Martians capable of building huge waterways that we could see from Earth?

Intrigued and excited, Lowell decided to build an observatory beneath the clearest skies he could find. He selected a site, which he named Mars Hill, in Flagstaff, Arizona. The observatory was completed and operational before October 1894, when Mars could be viewed especially

well. At that time, Mars was particularly close to Earth and "in opposition," which means it appeared on the opposite side of Earth from the Sun and remained visible throughout the night. In a speech Lowell made that year, he said that he hoped to make "an investigation into the condition of life on other worlds."

Lowell spent many years sketching what he saw when he pointed his powerful telescope at Mars. His maps included intricate drawings

Percival Lowell founded, designed, and built the Lowell Observatory in Flagstaff, Arizona.

of what he believed was a complex network of canals. Lowell published numerous newspaper articles and books about the canals and their builders. He concluded that the climate on Mars was extremely dry, so Martians had built an immense canal system to carry water from the planet's polar ice caps to drier regions near the equator. There, observers noticed dark areas that some believed were patches of vegetation irrigated by the canals.

Lowell's studies fired the imagination of people everywhere. They looked forward to hearing about his latest discoveries, just as people many years later eagerly followed the results of NASA planetary missions, such as the Mars Pathfinder and the Mars Global Surveyor Missions. In November 1909, the *Los Angeles Times* reported Lowell's discovery of several new canals on Mars. According to the article, "Professor Lowell says that he has found three or four new canals of recent making up there. 'These canals look to us like signs of intelligent, purposive work, rather than natural markings,' he said."

The structures that Lowell and Schiaparelli saw looked like long, continuous, connected constructions. Lowell used his imagination to hypothesize what those structures might be and what function they might serve, and he concluded they were artificially built canals. Maybe he jumped to conclusions too hastily, but his ideas aroused public interest in Mars. Many scientists disagreed with Lowell's claims, but the idea of canals on Mars intrigued the public as well as some groups of scientists for more than 50 years.

In 1924, a former astronomy professor named David Todd suggested that a recent invention—the radio—might allow people on Earth to hear Martian broadcasts. Todd reasoned

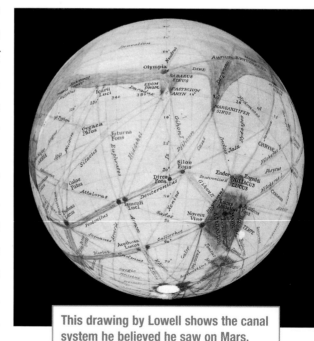

This drawing by Lowell shows the canal system he believed he saw on Mars.

that if an advanced civilization did exist on Mars, the Martians would certainly have invented radio transmitters. With luck, we might be able to pick up their signals.

Beginning on March 23, 1924, when Mars would make its closest approach to Earth since 1804, the United States Army and Navy agreed to listen for any strange signals. Radio stations in the United States were asked to stop broadcasting for 5 minutes every hour to avoid interference with Martian signals. Business was business, though. When the time came, only one station—WRC in Washington, D.C.—maintained silence.

The experiment ended in disappointment. A few crank phone calls and some static came in, but no radio signals from Mars were ever detected. Still, many people remained hopeful. A report in *The New York Times* predicted that humans ". . . would never cease trying to establish communication with Mars."

Martians in Fiction

English writer H. G. Wells was among the first to get fired up by reports of canals on Mars. In 1898, Wells published a frightening science-fiction novel called *War of the Worlds*. H. G. Wells was no relation to actor-director Orson Welles, but he did inspire the younger man. In the fantastic tale of *War of the Worlds*, Martians use deadly war machines to invade England—and they almost succeed in conquering our entire home planet. It was the first best-selling story about invaders from another world. It was also the first popular book to describe creatures from another world as monstrous warriors intent on conquering Earth.

Picking up from Lowell's theories, Wells depicted Mars as an old and dying planet. But in Wells's novel, the Martians, who look something

Great "War with Mars"

"**M**artian cylinders are falling all over the country!" The radio announcer who spoke seemed genuinely alarmed, especially to listeners who tuned in late to the *Mercury Theater* radio program on October 30, 1938. The "newsflash" that "interrupted the station's regular programming" said that Martians were invading the United States! Their weapon-bearing cylinders were falling in New Jersey; Buffalo, New York; Chicago, Illinois; and St. Louis, Missouri. The end seemed near.

Many people became hysterically frightened. Some people began to pack up and hurriedly leave their homes. Two people committed suicide. It wasn't until hours later that many people realized there was no Martian invasion. The "newsflash" was just part of a Halloween radio program. Unfortunately, many listeners believed the "announcement" made by actor and director Orson Welles. Percival Lowell's vision of elaborate canal systems and Martian cities had made a Martian invasion seem possible.

like ugly giant octopuses, have given up trying to save their planet with canals. Moving to another planet seems the best idea. But since they obviously believe Earth isn't big enough for everyone, they arrive with war machines packed inside giant, flying cylinders. A lot of action-packed thrills occur before a surprise ending saves the Earthlings from the Martians.

H. G. Wells wasn't the first writer to examine the possibilities of life on other worlds, however. Astronomer Johannes Kepler, who calculated the elliptical orbit of Mars, had published a book called *Somnium (Dreams)*. It describes a traveler who visits the Moon in a dream. In 1656, the French poet and adventurer Savinien de Cyrano de Bergerac published a book detailing a voyage to the Moon. H. G. Wells, though, built on the public's fascination with Mars, and he created a sensation.

Other writers were quick to follow in H. G. Wells's footsteps. In 1912, Edgar Rice Burroughs, creator of the Tarzan adventure books, wrote *Under the Moons of Mars*. It was the first in a series of books about the adventures of Captain John Carter, who finds himself mysteriously transported to the red planet. Burroughs's Martians looked and acted more like humans than those created by Wells, and Captain Carter's colorful adventures often involved romance, along with the usual thrills and danger.

The Burroughs novels about Mars had a tremendous following, especially among young readers. Such noted people as scientist Carl Sagan and science-fiction writer Ray Bradbury were inspired by the adventurous and imaginative stories.

Years later, Ray Bradbury wrote one of the best novels about Mars. Some people criticize Bradbury's book, *The Martian Chronicles* (1950), for its lack of accuracy, but the story is both poetic and haunting. Martians are presented as a lost and dying race, but, as people from Earth arrive to colonize the red planet, the beauties and mysteries of the ancient Martians and their way of life begin to affect Earthlings in unexpected ways.

Bradbury took a great deal of poetic

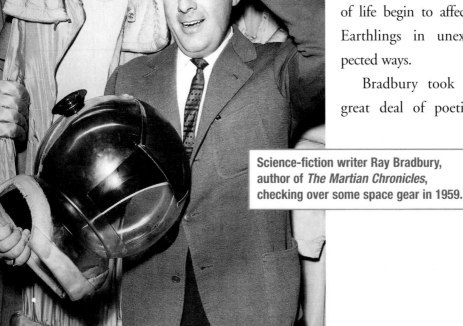

Science-fiction writer Ray Bradbury, author of *The Martian Chronicles*, checking over some space gear in 1959.

license in presenting his portrait of Mars and Martian life, as did several other authors, including C. S. Lewis in *Out of the Silent Planet* (1938) and Robert Heinlein in *Stranger in a Strange Land* (1961). Kim Stanley Robinson's *Red Mars* (1993), *Green Mars* (1995), and *Blue Mars* (1996) present more realistic portrayals of Mars. *Mars Underground* (1997), written by planetary scientist, writer, and painter William K. Hartmann, provides an extremely realistic visit to Mars.

Astronomical Artist: William Hartmann

William Hartmann is a planetary scientist and astronomer. He is also an artist—a painter of landscapes. There is something a bit unusual about Hartmann's landscapes, however. They depict scenes located millions—or even billions—of miles from Earth. He has painted views of all the planets in our solar system and their moons as well as asteroids, comets, and galaxies—all with the eye of an artist and the knowledge of an astronomer.

In 1997, Hartmann published his first novel. *Mars Underground* is the story of a human colony on Mars. Set in the year 2031, it is an exciting, yet realistic, view of what life might be like on the red planet.

A resident of Arizona, Hartmann knows the feel of a desert firsthand, and anyone reading his descriptions of the arid deserts and polar regions of Mars will have no trouble imagining the terrain of the red planet.

William Hartmann painted this image of astronauts exploring Phobos, one of Mars's two moons.

From Fiction to Fact

Eventually, scientists realized that the canals of Mars were simply the result of eyestrain and visual tricks played by the mind. However, Lowell's theories about the canals and his ideas about life on Mars seeded many fertile and imaginative minds. With only a few exceptions, most science-fiction stories portrayed life on Mars as definite and real.

We now know there is no advanced civilization on Mars. Still, many intriguing questions about our red-hued neighbor remain unanswered. It has been a long journey from our first glimpses of a rusty-red light in the night sky to the beginnings of a basic understanding of Mars. It has been a journey of both science and imagination, of fact and of fiction. Sometimes, admittedly, our fictions have far outpaced our facts.

Most of the factual information we now have about Mars has been collected since the 1960s. It has come from photos and data returned to Earth by space probes. Some of these spacecraft flew by Mars and then headed off into space; others orbited the planet; and still others landed on the Martian surface. Many more probes will be sent to Mars in the future. One day, humans may even visit the fourth planet from the Sun.

Spacecraft to Mars

Hopes were high in 1964, when a little spacecraft called *Mariner 4* began its journey to Mars. At last, scientists would get their first close-up view of the planet everyone was so curious about. As the spacecraft drew near to the red planet in July 1965, NASA engineers and scientists prepared to turn on the instruments. Everyone was anxious to see the mysterious surface of Mars. A few people even hoped to see one of Percival Lowell's canals, or some other sign of life on the red planet.

Finally, the pictures began to come in—twenty-two blurry images of a dismal expanse of rust-colored, desert-like surface covered with craters. Far from looking like the home of an advanced civilization, Mars appeared to be as lifeless and desolate as our own Moon. Even the atmosphere turned out to be much thinner than scientists expected.

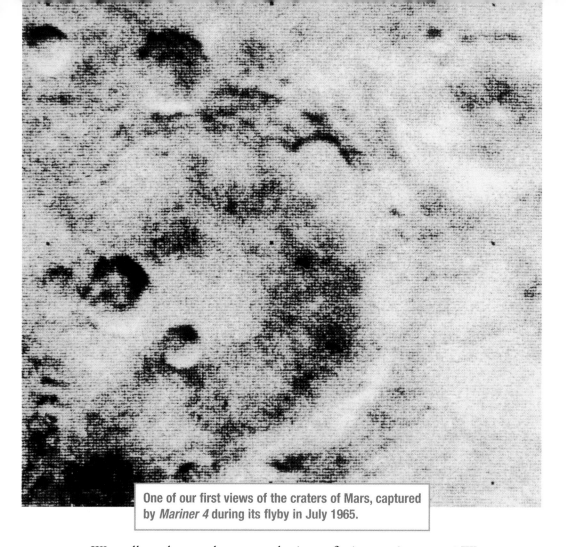

One of our first views of the craters of Mars, captured by *Mariner 4* during its flyby in July 1965.

Were all our hopes, dreams, and science-fiction stories wrong? Was Mars a dead planet, both geologically and biologically? Had we achieved all the exciting developments of the Space Age only to make such a disappointing discovery?

The Race for Mars

Early in the Space Age, sending a spacecraft to Mars had become a primary goal among scientists, science-fiction fans, the intellectually curious, and even politicians.

In the late 1950s, space exploration had developed into a kind of race between the United States and the former Soviet Union, which included present-day Russia, Ukraine, and several other countries in eastern Europe. The United States and the Soviet Union—also called the Union of Soviet Socialist Republics (USSR)—were unfriendly, but not technically at war. After World War II, they had entered a period called the "Cold War." During that time, each country stockpiled nuclear weapons and competed ferociously for worldwide esteem. The governments of both countries reasoned that superior rockets and technology in space would translate into respect for their military power on Earth. So a "space race" began.

In 1957, the USSR launched *Sputnik*, the first artificial satellite sent into Earth orbit. Never before had any nation sent an object so high. In 1961, the USSR launched the first human being—Yuri Gagarin—into space. Both the United States and the Soviet Union had already begun sending unmanned missions to the Moon and Venus.

The path to the red planet was full of pitfalls, though. Beginning in 1960, the Soviet Union made several attempts to send probes to Mars, but each one failed. The first mission sent by the United States, *Mariner 3* in 1964, also failed. The solar panels that were supposed to power the craft never opened, and *Mariner 3* ended its days circling the Sun aimlessly.

Finally, though, *Mariner 4* made it. The little spacecraft reached Mars in July 1965 and sent back the very first close-up views. The mission was a success but, unfortunately, the results disappointed most people. The next two U.S. flyby missions, *Mariner 6* and *Mariner 7*, also succeeded. Both reached Mars in 1969, and each one sent back a

An artist's conception of the design of *Mariner 6* and *Mariner 7*, twin spacecraft that flew by Mars a few days apart in 1969.

few photos of other areas of the Martian surface. Most of the planet was still a mystery.

The Soviet Union continued to launch spacecraft, but most never made it to the red planet. Other Soviet spacecraft sent back interesting data from Venus and the Moon, but Mars seemed to elude them. American politicians may have cheered at each of their rival's failures—the more the Soviets failed, the better the United States looked—but these losses prevented us from learning more about Mars.

The year 1971 was a great one for Mars watchers. In May, three missions roared off the launch pads—two Soviet missions, *Mars 2* and *Mars 3*, and one U.S. mission, *Mariner 9*. They were not all complete successes, however. *Mars 2* and *Mars 3* each consisted of two parts—an orbiter and a lander. Although both orbiters reached Mars and went into orbit without a hitch, the landers did not fare so well. The *Mars 2* lander crashed into the planet, and the *Mars 3* lander transmitted pictures for only 20 seconds before fizzling out.

At first, the results from NASA's *Mariner 9* seemed disappointing, too. For weeks after the spacecraft arrived, we saw nothing but whirling dust on the surface of Mars. The probe had reached the planet in the middle of a giant dust storm.

Land of Giant Mountains and Vast Valleys

Eventually, though, the dust began to clear, and scientists could see three rounded bumps sticking up above the swirling clouds. These were the first sign of all the surprises *Mariner 9* had in store for us. The bumps turned out to be the flattened summits of three giant volcanoes located in the region of Mars called Tharsis.

Through the eyes of *Mariner 9*, scientists discovered that Mars is a complex world with many kinds of terrain. The probe showed that Mars is not only a planet of frigid desert landscapes, but also a world of towering mountains, giant valleys, and vast plains.

For the first time, scientists saw indications that large amounts of water had once flowed across the surface of Mars. By the time *Mariner 9* completed its year-long mission, scientists had received 7,329 pictures, and their view of Mars had completely changed. The spacecraft had mapped 85 percent of the Martian surface and had sent back the first photos of the Martian moons—Phobos and Deimos. Suddenly, Mars had become much more interesting—even without canals!

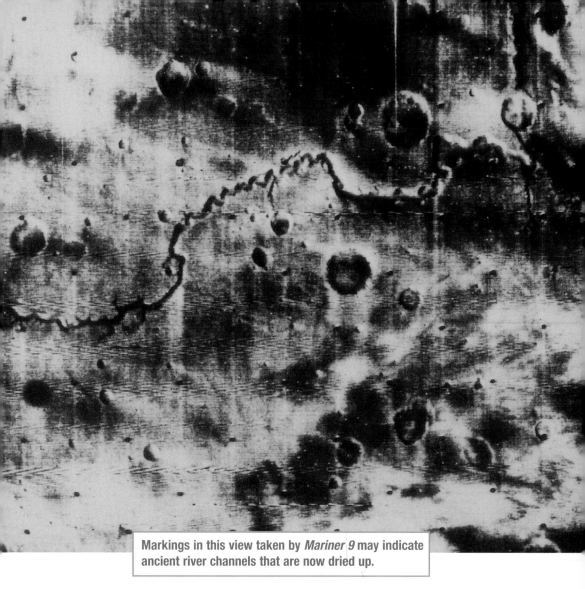

Markings in this view taken by *Mariner 9* may indicate ancient river channels that are now dried up.

First Ground-Level View

Many, many questions remained, and not the least of them was: Is there life on Mars? By this time, no one expected to find Martian cities, but perhaps some bacteria lived in the soil. With this and other questions in mind, NASA designed the Viking mission, which consisted of two spacecraft—*Viking 1* and *Viking 2.*

A Viking mission sets off for Mars

Viking 1 lifted off from Kennedy Space Center in Cape Canaveral, Florida, in August 1975. *Viking 2* left a month later. Each spacecraft included two parts—an orbiter that would circle the planet and relay communications to Earth and a lander that would parachute to the surface and run tests from the ground.

On July 20, 1976, the *Viking 1* lander set down gently in a region called Chryse Planitia, which means "Plains of Gold," and began sending scientists the first photographs of Mars taken at ground level. Scientists saw a vast, bleak, rusty-red plain stretching out as far as the cameras could show. Rippling dunes of red sand were strewn with rocks and boulders beneath a salmon-colored sky. The color of the sky

The first color photo taken of the Martian surface by *Viking 1*

was a particular surprise—scientists had assumed the color would be deep blue. Instead, the sky on Mars is orangish-pink, tinged by the reflection of sunlight off the reddish dust particles in the thin Martian atmosphere.

A few months later, in September, the *Viking 2* lander touched down in an area called Utopia Planitia, which means "Utopian Plains." Its photographs showed scientists a rolling plain with few sand dunes.

Both landers sent back color panoramas of Martian sunsets and sunrises. They took a total of 4,500 images, while the orbiters took 52,000 more.

After completing their scheduled experiments, the Viking landers became weather stations and continued to record and transmit for many years. They recorded temperatures—the lowest was –184 degrees Fahrenheit (–120 degrees Celsius) and the highest was 7°F (–14°C). They measured wind speeds of near-hurricane strength. They analyzed the atmosphere and observed high, swirling clouds and

How Science Works: Looking for Life on Mars

The Viking landers arrived on Mars equipped and programmed to search for life on the red planet. Measurements of the soil showed that ultraviolet radiation from the Sun saturated the surface at extremely high levels. In addition, the soil was remarkably dry—except for a thin layer of water frost in the winter near the *Viking 2* lander—and so chemically active it would probably destroy any delicate organic molecules that might form there.

The landers also carried instruments designed to detect organic molecules in the soil. These instruments looked for signs of metabolism, growth, and photosynthesis. The results of these experiments puzzled scientists. They found unexpected chemical activity in the Martian soil, but there was no clear evidence of living microorganisms near either of the landing sites. Scientists concluded that the Martian soil was sterile.

patches of early morning fog. The last Viking lander transmission reached Earth in November 1982. The Viking missions may have provided no evidence of life on Mars, but they gave us a great deal of valuable information.

In honor of the man who led the Viking lander imaging team, the *Viking 1* landing site has been renamed the Thomas A. Mutch Memorial Station. A plaque with this information is now in the custody of the National Air and Space Museum in Washington, D.C. If all goes according to plan, members of a manned expedition to Mars will one day hang the plaque on the *Viking 1* lander, which still rests on the surface of the red planet.

The Ones that Got Away

Following the Viking successes of 1976, came a few failures. In July 1988, the USSR launched twin spacecraft to the Martian moon Phobos, but both went astray. Four years later, the United States launched a mapping probe called *Mars Observer*. The launch went smoothly, and the spacecraft seemed fine as it cruised toward Mars. Then, suddenly, in August 1993, just as it was about to enter orbit, mission controllers on Earth lost contact with the spacecraft.

No one knows exactly what happened to *Mars Observer*. Some evidence suggests that an electronic circuit failed. In any case, communication broke down and, unguided, it probably veered off course and disappeared into space.

For Mars watchers, the loss of these three spacecraft came as a tremendous blow. These missions all held promise and many people were eager to find learn more about Mars and its moons. The price tag was also very high, however, and the Cold War was over. In 1991, the USSR broke up into more than a dozen countries, and politicians no longer had a "space race" to justify the cost of going to Mars.

From that point on, the best reason for sending spacecraft to Mars was to learn more about it. If the red planet had indeed been similar to Earth at one time, why had it turned out so differently? Most of all, we still wanted to know what lay over the next hill or around the next bend. We had a longing to explore and to understand.

Mars *Pathfinder*: A Big Bounce and a Little Robot

With these goals in mind, NASA launched *Mars Pathfinder* in December 1996. It was part of a series of innovative missions designed to explore the planets and their moons. *Pathfinder* was the first craft ever to land on a planet's surface without first going into orbit.

Three triangular panels enclosed the pyramid-shaped lander as it sped toward the Martian surface. A system of parachutes and rockets helped slow its fall, but the most important features were the giant airbags that enclosed the spacecraft like a cocoon and allowed it to bounce when it landed. During impact, the lander bounced fifteen or twenty times before it finally came to rest. Meanwhile, NASA scientists and engineers held their breath—this was an important test of a daring new approach to spacecraft landing—one that required much less fuel.

After landing, the craft's airbags deflated and its three triangular panels unfolded—like the petals of a flower—onto the ground, just as planned. For the rest of the mission, the panels provided solar power for the trusty little ground station. So far, all was well.

A photo of a *Pathfinder* test on Earth, showing the airbags that would cushion its landing on Mars and then fold out of the way as the lander's petals opened.

Managing Mars Exploration: Donna Shirley

When Donna Shirley was a child, she loved science fiction and longed to go to Mars. As an adult, she did the next-best thing—she managed the Mars Exploration Program at NASA's Jet Propulsion Laboratory (JPL) in Pasadena, California. While she was in charge, *Pathfinder* and the rover *Sojourner* traveled to Mars. She also oversaw the development of three flight projects and directed studies for many future missions to Mars.

Surprisingly, Shirley says her worst subject in school was math. She wanted to be an aeronautical engineer, though, so she kept at it until she got it. When she went to college, her advisor told her, "Girls can't be engineers!" But Donna Shirley didn't let that stop her. She says, "I told him I could, and I did!" Before she was through, Shirley had earned two bachelor's degrees—one in engineering and the other in journalism—and a master's degree in aeronautical engineering.

Shirley's first job at JPL involved studying what would happen when a spacecraft lander descends to the surface of Mars. How would the Martian atmosphere affect the movement of the lander? How could the lander survive without burning up? How could the engineers keep it from tumbling out of control? The job was a real challenge, but a strong technical education, flexibility, and hard work were the keys to Shirley's success.

Thirty years later, Shirley was managing the whole program. Donna Shirley has now retired from JPL, but NASA officials still sometimes ask her for advice. She has also written the book *Managing Martians* about her experiences building teams of talented people who could work well together.

Donna Shirley poses with a model of *Sojourner.*

Inside *Pathfinder* was a little robot rover about the size of a microwave oven, directed by remote control from Earth. Named *Sojourner* after Sojourner Truth (one of the first African-American women to speak out against slavery), the little six-wheeled vehicle struggled out of its berth aboard *Pathfinder*. The men and women in the NASA control room watched, along with millions of television viewers, as *Sojourner* rolled slowly and carefully down its ramp, paused briefly, and then dropped off onto Martian soil.

The time delay of 6 to 41 minutes between the controller's signal from Earth and the rover's reaction made for some agonizing moments. As *Sojourner* rolled across the Martian surface, it performed experiments on some of the rocks it passed. Scientists gave these rocks such playful names as Barnacle Bill, Yogi, and Scooby-Doo. The final signal from *Sojourner* was heard on Earth on September 27, 1997. The intrepid little scout had done its job and done it well.

Less Is More?

The glories of 1997 were not over yet. *Mars Global Surveyor*, launched in September 1996, took a slower route than *Pathfinder* and arrived in Mars orbit on September 12, 1997. On board was the Mars Orbiter Camera, which had been designed—at least in part—to put to rest some controversies about Mars. We'll discuss these findings in the next chapter.

In its first year, the *Mars Global Surveyor* mission took some spectacular images while it slowed down to its ultimate tight, circular orbit close to the planet. Initially, the spacecraft's orbit was highly eccentric, looping close to the planet and then moving farther out. Each time the

Successful Missions to Mars

Vital Statistics

Spacecraft	Date of Launch	Date of Arrival at Mars	Sponsor Country
MARINER 4	November 28, 1964	July 14, 1965	U.S.
MARINER 6	February 24, 1969	July 31, 1969	U.S.
MARINER 7	March 27, 1969	August 5, 1969	U.S.
MARS 2	May 19, 1971	November 27, 1971	USSR
MARS 3	May 28, 1971	December 2, 1971	USSR
MARINER 9	May 30, 1971	November 13, 1971	U.S.
MARS 5	July 25, 1973	February 2, 1974	USSR
MARS 6	August 5, 1973	March 12, 1974	USSR
VIKING 1	August 20, 1975	July 19, 1976 (Mars orbit); July 20 (lander sets down on the surface)	U.S.
VIKING 2	September 9, 1975	September 3, 1976	U.S.
PHOBOS 2	July 12, 1988	January 30, 1989	USSR
MARS GLOBAL SURVEYOR	November 7, 1996	September 12, 1997	U.S.
MARS PATHFINDER	December 4, 1996	July 4, 1997	U.S.

spacecraft came close to Mars, it skimmed through the atmosphere in a process called *aerobraking* to slow the craft's speed and lower its orbit. Beginning in March 1999, *Mars Global Surveyor* moved into the mapping phase of its mission. By May 2000, NASA had posted more than 20,000 *Surveyor* images of Mars on the Internet for the public to view. Many included rocks and other features the size of a schoolbus. These images showed Mars as a truly bizarre and alien place.

NASA planned two more missions to arrive during the last months of 1999, the *Mars Climate Orbiter* and the *Mars Polar Lander*. Everyone hoped for more exciting results. However, this time things did not go so well. The mission team for the *Mars Climate Orbiter* lost touch with the spacecraft just as it entered orbit to begin its weather reports. As the *Mars Polar Lander* descended towards the surface to study the Martian soil, it also stopped communicating. Many people thought political pressures had pushed the scientists and engineers too hard for "faster, better, cheaper" missions. Managing a space mission is a complex process involving thousands of details, and the mission teams need to have the time and resources to give the missions the care they deserve.

More missions are planned for Mars, though, and their planners will learn from the 1999 losses. In the meantime, Mars scientists have a wealth of exciting information to study from *Mars Global Surveyor*.

Chapter 4

Getting to Know Mars

Imagine you are about to take an incredible journey across the surface of Mars in a human-sized rover vehicle. You notice an unusual spring in your step as you walk toward the rover, and it isn't only because you're going to take such an exciting trip. Mars has only one-third the gravity of Earth, so you weigh a lot less on Mars than you do on Earth.

You'll need sunglasses to protect your eyes from the Sun's harsh UV radiation and the planet's glaring, orange-pink sky. You will also need a large supply of oxygen to breathe and a space suit to protect yourself against the low atmospheric pressure and UV radiation. Temperatures on the Martian surface will be very cold, so be sure to bring your thermal underwear.

You should also be prepared for windy conditions. Measurements at both Viking lander sites showed steady, daily winds of about 8 to 16 miles (15 to 25 km) per hour, with full-force gales of more than 89 miles (143 km) per hour during dust storms that envelop the planet each spring and summer. Images captured by the Pathfinder mission show evidence of tornadolike, high-speed "dust devils" that cause soil erosion on Mars.

As you begin your trip at the *Viking 1* landing site, everything you see has a rusty color, and much of the surrounding landscape is strewn with jagged chunks of rock ranging in size from tiny pebbles to huge boulders. Looking out across the terrain, you see a series of tall dunes made of very fine, powdery dust. The same dust peppers the tops of rocks nearby and drifts between them, as if blown by the planet's strong wind. The surface of Mars seems strange, desolate, and desert-like.

The Birth of a Planet

Before you hop into the rover and begin your trip, you need to take a few moments to learn a little background information about the history of our solar system and the formation of the planets.

About 4.5 billion years ago, in our region of the galaxy, a vast cloud of whirling dust and gas began to collapse and condense into a huge, flattened disk. At the center of this rapidly collapsing material, the temperatures became so high that *fusion* began to take place. This produced enough energy and outward pressure to stop the material from contracting further. A star—our Sun—had been born.

At nearly the same time, smaller clumps of dust and gas began to form close to the Sun. These clumps were not big enough to become

An artist's conception of the formation of the solar system

stars, so they condensed into *planetesimals*—the beginnings of planets, moons, *comets*, and *asteroids*.

Three of these planets were quite similar in size and composition and were surrounded by atmospheres of gas. They were close to the Sun, but not too close. Although these three planets—Venus, Earth,

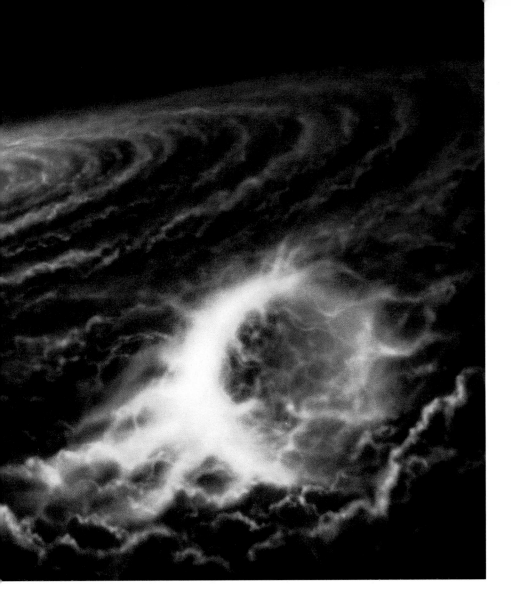

and Mars—may have been "born triplets," they began to change at some point. Today the three planets are totally unlike one another. Mars is cold and dry, and its atmosphere is thin. Yet, scientists see many signs of a far different past. At one time, water flowed across surface of the red planet, and the basic ingredients of life were present.

Mars is one of the four *terrestrial*, or rocky, planets. Mercury, Venus, and Earth are also terrestrial planets. Unlike the *gas giants* in the outer solar system, a terrestrial planet has a partial record of its history preserved on its surface. When erupting volcanoes spread hot lava over its surface or *meteoroids* crash into it, they leave behind a visible history—while at the same time destroying parts of the previous record. Geologists use the clues on a planet's surface to learn about its history.

Our Moon and Mercury show few, if any, signs of geological activity. So they provide scientists with undisturbed records of events that happened up to 3 billion years ago. The surfaces of Venus and Earth are considerably younger. Much of Venus's surface may be less than 500 million years old.

On Earth, flowing lava and residue from floods constantly renew the surface, while earthquakes reorganize it. Wind, rain, rivers, and oceans erode Earth's layers. The crust beneath the ocean is very young—only about 200 million years old.

Unlike Mars, Venus is shrouded by clouds, which cover its relatively young surface.

Scientists can find a record of Earth's first billion years in only a few remote places on our planet.

On Mars, scientists have found some old records as well as some newer ones.

Inside Mars

Scientists don't know much about the interior regions of Mars, but they are reasonably sure that, like Earth, Mars has three layers: an inner *core* at the center, a *mantle* in the middle, and an exterior crust. As Mars, and most other objects in the solar system formed, large quantities of energy and heat were produced.

Wind, rain, rivers, and oceans erode the layers of Earth's surface.

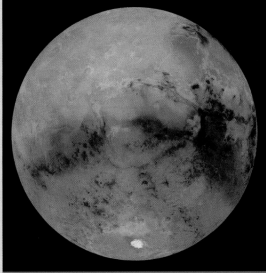

Lava from huge volcanoes in Mars's Tharsis region (upper left) have renewed some parts of the surface.

The southern regions of Mars have very ancient terrain covered with craters. Near the equator, in an area known as the Tharsis bulge, huge volcanoes stand as evidence of continual eruptions that may have taken place throughout the planet's history. In addition, shifts in the planet's crust have combined with wind, ice, and water to reshape various parts of the Martian surface.

As Earth, Mars, and other bodies heated up, their interiors melted and *differentiation* took place. That is, denser materials sank to form a core in the center, while less dense materials rose toward the surface, forming a mantle and crust.

The center of Earth consists primarily of iron and nickel. Because Mars is farther from the Sun, it did not heat up quite as much as Earth.

As a result, scientists believe that Mars's core may consist primarily of sulfur and copper. If this is true, the Martian mantle and crust should contain little evidence of these materials. The findings of scientists who study *meteorites* from Mars support this theory. One day, scientists hope to be able to test this hypothesis on rock samples taken directly from Mars.

Continuing Your Journey

As you travel across the face of Mars in your rover, you may not be impressed when you first come to the great *shield volcano* Olympus Mons. Although it is huge, your rover can easily climb the gradual 2 percent grade. It would probably take quite a while to realize that you were climbing a monster mountain.

Olympus Mons is so enormous that its base would cover the entire state of Missouri, and it stands 16.8 miles (27 km) high. A gaping hole at its crest measures nearly 50 miles (80 km) across. Nothing on Earth even approaches this size. The world's highest mountain, Mount Everest, rises only about 5.5 miles (8.9 km) above sea level. The shield volcano Mauna Loa in Hawaii measures about 74.6 miles (120 km) across and stands 5.6 miles (9 km) above the ocean floor.

Although Mars is smaller than Earth, nearly everything on the Martian surface is grand in scale. About 932 miles (1,500 km) southeast of Olympus Mons, the three shield volcanoes first spied by *Mariner 9* are only slightly smaller. They are flat on top and jut out of Tharsis bulge like enormous slabs of rock.

Volcanoes must have played an important role in the development of Mars's atmosphere. At one time, they belched huge quantities of carbon dioxide and water vapor into the air. During their most active periods, they probably warmed the planet's surface considerably.

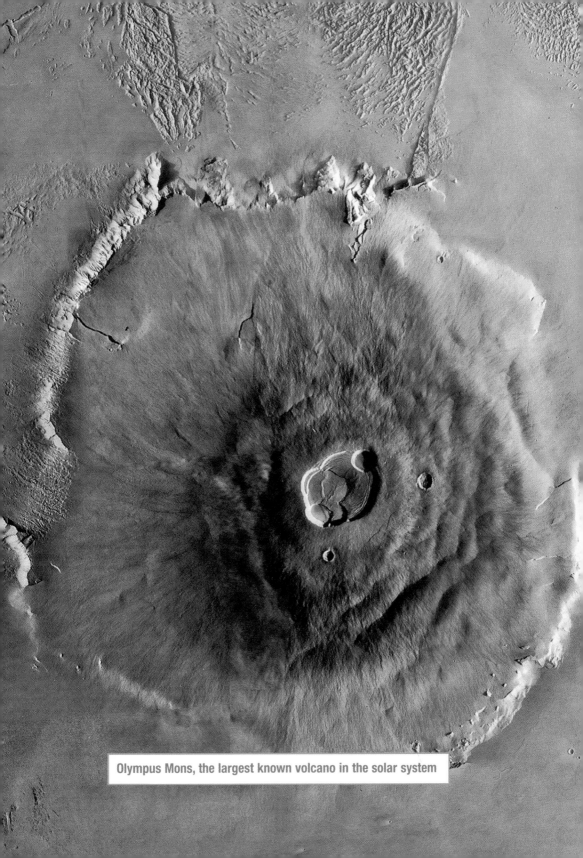

Olympus Mons, the largest known volcano in the solar system

Many planetologists think these volcanoes are no longer active, but other experts disagree. For example, Michael Carr of the U.S. Geological Survey believes the volcanoes on Mars may still erupt. Images taken by the *Mars Global Surveyor* seem to back him up. Some of the lava spills in these pictures appear to be relatively recent.

Because Mars has no mountain ranges or evidence of faults, until recently, most scientists thought that Mars is too small to have a crust divided into sheets of rock called *tectonic plates*. Earth has six very large tectonic plates and about a dozen smaller ones. At places where the edges of two plates meet, they either push against each other or pull apart. When two plates push against each other, one plate slides under the other one and melts to become part of Earth's mantle. These movements create massive tensions that cause earthquakes and volcanoes and, over millions of years, form mountain ranges and rift valleys.

In 1999, the magnetometer on board *Mars Global Surveyor* made a surprising discovery—invisible bands of magnetic fields on the surface of Mars. These magnetic bands are similar to patterns seen in the crust of Earth's seafloors where gaps or edges of tectonic plates occur and the crust is continually renewed. Close examination of the magnetic bands on Mars indicates that the red planet may have once had the same kind of seething, fluid interior as Earth has today. Scientists believe that—perhaps because of its small size—Mars's tectonic activity came to an end long ago.

Vast Valleys and Colossal Canyons

If you think Olympus Mons is impressive, you will be astounded by a visit to Valles Marineris. It makes the Grand Canyon in Colorado look like an irrigation ditch in your vegetable garden. Laid out across the

United States, Valles Marineris would stretch from New York City to Los Angeles. It is 124 miles (200 km) wide and up to 4.3 miles (7 km) deep—more than three times as deep as the Grand Canyon.

The western end of Valles Marineris begins at the Tharsis bulge. This huge system of valleys and canyons stretches thousands of miles eastward and ends in a jumbled, chaotic terrain. Geologists think the western end of this huge gash across the middle of Mars was caused by

The great canyon Valles Marineris cuts across the surface of Mars. The three giant volcanoes of Tharsis are visible as dark red spots near the top of this photo.

tectonic stresses so severe that they split open the planet's crust. The middle portion of Valles Marineris shows evidence of catastrophic flooding, with drainage channels running to the north. The eastern end of the huge valley system probably formed when a portion of the overlying surface collapsed.

The Valles Marineris is only the grandest of many huge Martian channels that offer convincing evidence that water once gushed over the land. Many of these channels, such as Ravi Vallis, spring up suddenly from nowhere. Ravi Vallis was clearly caused by an enormous outflow of liquid water from the planet's interior. The floors of Mars's channels show signs of scouring, and teardrop-shaped islands remain where water flowed around obstacles in its path.

Most of these huge channels flow to the northern plains, where they empty into an enormous basin area. Spacecraft images also show conventional drainage systems with tributaries that flow into larger riverbeds, and finally into the northern plains.

The Atmosphere on Mars

The rover transporting you across the Martian surface has a large supply of oxygen on board. It's a good thing, too, because humans can't breathe on Mars. Earth's thick atmosphere consists primarily of nitrogen and oxygen, while the thin atmosphere of Mars is composed almost entirely of carbon dioxide.

What exactly is atmosphere? Basically, it is a collection of gases that escaped from within a planet as it cooled. It is held in place by gravity. The exact makeup of a planet's atmosphere depends on many factors, including the planet's size, composition, and temperature.

The gravity of a massive planet such as Jupiter can hold a huge atmosphere, and even Earth's weaker gravity has been able to hold

The giant planet Jupiter has a huge atmosphere.

onto large amounts of nitrogen, some oxygen, and trace amounts of a few other gases. Methane, hydrogen, and ammonia—lighter gases that once formed part of Earth's atmosphere—escaped into space long ago.

Mars is about half the size of Earth and has one-tenth of its mass, so its gravitational pull is much weaker than Earth's. As a result, most of Mars's gases escaped as its interior cooled. Some of the oxygen from the planet's primitive atmosphere combined with iron on its surface, producing the planet's rusty-red color. Except for a thin layer of carbon dioxide, all Mars's other gases drifted off into space long ago.

At one time, Mars probably had a thick atmosphere. Today, only a thin layer of carbon dioxide surrounds the red planet.

Billions of years ago, Mars was a very different place. Volcanoes on its surface belched gases and steam, creating a thick atmosphere composed of water vapor and carbon dioxide. As the sunlight hit the planet's surface, it was reflected and then absorbed and trapped by carbon dioxide in the atmosphere. The result was a *greenhouse effect* similar to the one we experience on Earth. Over time, the planet warmed and water was able to exist in a liquid state.

While plants and animals probably never existed on Mars, many scientists think that some forms of life may have thrived in the Martian greenhouse. As we have seen on Earth, where there's liquid water, there is usually life.

Where Did All the Water Go?

As you have learned, Earth's thick atmosphere traps heat from the Sun. Winds and water currents circulate that heat around the globe. As a result, temperatures on Earth don't vary nearly as much as they do on Mars. On Earth, the air temperature drops only a little at night. On Mars, the air temperature may drop as much as 100°F (54°C) at night.

Because temperatures on Earth are fairly constant from day to night and from season to season, most of the water on our planet exists as a liquid all the time. This is not the case on Mars. Although the planet once had large quantities of liquid water, today that water is gone.

Where did all the water go? Most likely, some of the water vapor and carbon dioxide in Mars's atmosphere escaped into space. Less carbon dioxide meant a weaker greenhouse effect. As temperatures on Mars cooled, most of the liquid water froze. Some of it became locked in polar ice caps beneath the layer of frozen carbon dioxide.

In 1998, *Mars Global Surveyor* transmitted images of the northern polar region back to Earth. This area of the planet consists of a depressed basin about one and a half times the size of Texas. It is amazingly flat in some areas and riddled with canyons in others. The mass of polar ice shown in the images looks a lot like a hockey puck sitting in a shallow bowl.

The northern polar region of Mars, as pictured by *Mars Global Surveyor*.

Scientists were surprised by the size of the ice cap. It contains about ten times less ice than they had predicted. If this area of the planet contains less water than expected, could more water be hiding elsewhere on the red planet? Perhaps some is tied up as permafrost in the top layers of soil, as it is in the tundra areas of northern Canada, Alaska, and Siberia. Also, large quantities of water may still be frozen underground. It is even possible that great seas of liquid water lie deep within the planet's interior.

Although scientists have a great deal to learn about what happened to Mars's water, they are certain of a few things. They know that, at one time, a great deal of water once existed on Mars, and that some remains there still. Because water is one of the prerequisites for life as we know it, Mars is, according to Stanford University geophysicist Norman H. Sleep, "a beautiful place to look for life." So the idea that life may once have existed on Mars, and may even exist there today, remains actively under investigation.

Chapter 5

The Search for Life Continues

As you have seen, the *canali* of Giovanni Schiaparelli and Percival Lowell touched a chord in the public mind long ago. Ever since, the idea of life on Mars has captivated us.

So far, though, it has been hard to find solid evidence that either proves or disproves whether life exists on Mars. In the middle and late nineteenth century, many people were convinced that long, continuous canals ran across the Martian surface. Some observers on Earth even thought they saw green vegetation on Mars, especially in the spring. As it turned out, both the "green" areas and the "canals" were optical illusions. Because much of the planet looks red from Earth, the contrasting dark areas look like green patches. In the spring, dust storms intensify the effect.

A color-enhanced view of Mars showing dark patches

Why did Mars watchers see canals? As they peered through Earth's thick atmosphere, their eyes saw discontinuous structures through their telescopes. Because their minds filled in what their eyes could not quite make out, they thought they saw channels or canals. As telescope technology improved, astronomers had more difficulty seeing Lowell's canals. When scientists took a look at images from *Mariner 4*, it was obvious that canals do not exist on Mars.

The "Face on Mars": Now You See It, Now You Don't

Remarkably, the Mariner images did not convince everyone. Some people continued to believe that evidence of an advanced civilization might still be found on Mars. Perhaps, then, it is not surprising that an image from the Viking missions touched off a new controversy in 1976.

The image showed a large shape in the Cydonia region of Mars's northern hemisphere. Some people claimed that it was a giant sculpture of a humanlike face carved either by Martians or by visitors from another, far-off planet. A few years later, computer scientists working for a NASA contractor enhanced the image and thought they also saw pyramid structures nearby. They concluded on their own—without really knowing anything about the subject—that the objects were not natural, and they published a book about their ideas.

By the 1980s, a science journalist named Richard Hoagland claimed he saw evidence of a giant construction project by intelligent beings. From there, highly speculative ideas began flying fast. Hoagland thought he saw nearby cities. The face was built—like Stonehenge, he thought—to point to the Sun at the time of the Martian solstice half a million years ago.

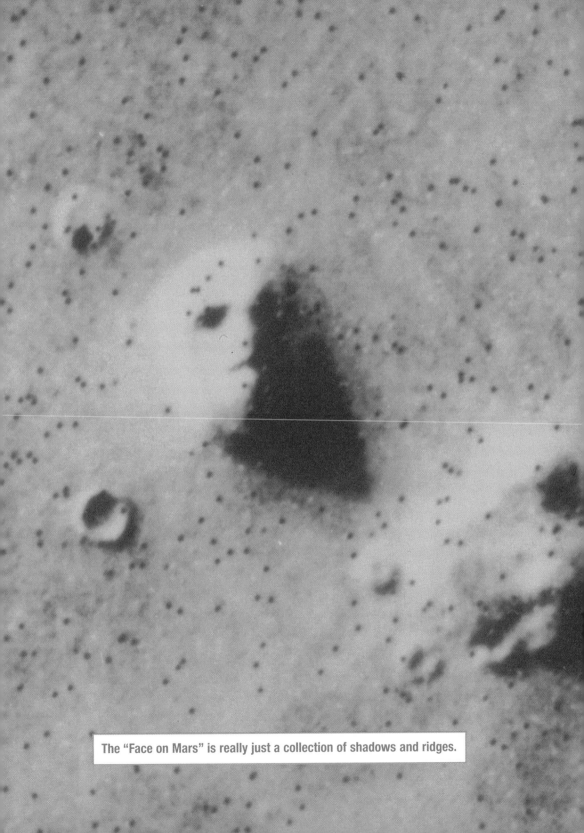

The "Face on Mars" is really just a collection of shadows and ridges.

People wondered why the face looked human, and Hoagland offered answers. Perhaps evolution had produced creatures on Mars that resembled humans on Earth. Maybe an unknown, technologically advanced civilization from Earth had traveled to Mars long ago. Or maybe we are actually descended from Martians who traveled here. Hoagland even suggested that the face was built by extraterrestrials who came from another solar system. Perhaps it was some kind of sign or test for us.

Geologists, however, felt certain that the structure was a natural phenomenon. The final evidence came in 1998, when *Mars Global Surveyor* took a straight-down image of the area surrounding the "Face on Mars." It was composed of natural hills and valleys in an eroded

Occam's Razor

While stories about the "Face on Mars" may be intriguing, Hoagland had no evidence to back up his claims. As the famous scientist Carl Sagan often remarked, extraordinary claims require extraordinary proof. Hoagland could not prove anything.

Before long, the "Face on Mars" had moved into the realm of pseudoscience, alongside stories about the so-called Bermuda Triangle, aliens at Roswell, New Mexico, and the Loch Ness Monster. Pseudoscience *seems* scientific because it often uses the language of science, but it doesn't hold up under close scrutiny. While Hoagland's speculations sold a lot of books, scientists didn't take him seriously.

Even before we had solid proof from the *Mars Global Surveyor*, scientists were quite certain that the "Face" was a natural structure. As Percival Lowell's experience shows, people can easily find themselves seeing what they want to see, especially when looking at an alien landscape. We've all seen the "Man in the Moon." If you stare at the Canadian flag, you can see the faces of two people on either side of the maple leaf. The human eye is easily fooled.

In evaluating stories like Hoagland's, a scientific principle called "Occam's razor" is a good guideline to keep in mind. According to William of Occam, a fourteenth-century English philosopher, when two explanations fit the evidence equally well, the simpler one is usually closer to the truth.

mesa. In reality, the "Face on Mars" is a low, oblong-shaped hill about 1 mile (1.6 km) long. When it is lit from the side by the late afternoon sunlight, it juts out from the surrounding terrain and is marked by what appear to be somber eyes, a nose, and a gaping mouth.

Looking for Signs of Life

Is there life on Mars? Today the planet has a thin atmosphere and is continually bombarded with ultraviolet radiation from the Sun. The surface is so cold that water remains frozen most of the year. When the Viking landers tested the soil for evidence of life forms, they came up empty-handed. Yet, despite these negative indicators, some scientists are not yet convinced.

Some Viking mission scientists are not certain that their experiments ruled out the possibility of life in the Martian soil. It is also possible that microorganisms exist in protected areas on the surface—cracks and crevices that contain some water and are not exposed to the Sun's intense radiation.

Where should we look for life on Mars then? What are the best sites for missions to achieve this purpose? *Exobiologists*—biologists who specialize in the search for life on other worlds—say the polar ice caps would be a good place to start. The frigid temperatures of these areas could make them promising deep freezes for living organisms. After all, scientists have found 3.5 million-year-old microorganisms still alive, though dormant, in the permafrost of Siberia, at 15°F (–9°C). The Martian polar caps are even colder—a steady –95°F (–71°C) throughout the planet's history. These lower temperatures could preserve microorganisms even more successfully than the Siberian permafrost, and we might still be able to find traces of them there.

Even if there are currently no living organisms on Mars, most scientists agree that life may have existed on Mars in the past. To find fossilized traces of these creatures, scientists would like to take a close look at the planet's dried lakebeds and areas where hot springs once flowed. The sediments that collected on lake bottoms billions of years ago could have trapped and preserved fossil organisms.

Mars's hot springs formed when sizzling hot water poured out of the planet's depths and quickly cooled as it neared the surface. This cooling would have caused minerals to settle out, taking organisms along for the ride and then preserving them as fossils. The water in hot springs would have remained liquid long after all other water on Mars was frozen solid because heat coming from deep within the planet would have kept them warm.

Martians in Antarctica?

In August 1996, a group of NASA scientists made a startling announcement about a meteorite found in Allan Hills ice field in Antarctica in 1984. Led by scientist David McKay, they concluded that this meteorite, known by the not-so-jazzy name of ALH84001, contained strong evidence that it had come here from Mars and contained microscopic signs of life. (The name ALH84001, by the way, tells us the place and date of its discovery: ALH for Allan Hills; 84 for 1984. The number 001 tells us it was the first meteorite found that year.)

The NASA team who studied the meteorite saw structures in the rock that could have been caused by very small living organisms—

Rock Man: Jack Farmer

Jack Farmer loved rocks when he was a child. He started collecting them when he was 6 years old. His mom gave him egg cartons to store his rocks in, and encouraged him to pursue his dreams.

In college, Farmer studied geology, and now he's an *exobiologist*. Farmer's wife, Maria, calls one end of their house the "Smithsonian Wing" because Farmer keeps a huge collection of strange and wonderful things there.

Farmer has done a lot of work for NASA on a type of ancient rock called stromatolite, which is consists of thin layers of sediment laid down by communities of microorganisms. He has collected samples up to 3.5 billion years old in Australia.

Farmer wants to know what the world was like when the organisms in these ancient rocks were alive. By understanding what early Earth was like, Farmer believes scientists may learn how life began on Earth. They may also develop better ways to search for evidence of ancient life on Mars.

Farmer has many interests. He is one-quarter Native American, and he enjoys studying the culture and history of his tribes, the Cherokee and Chickasaw. He has made and plays a rawhide drum. He also plays the Native American flute and the guitar. He even writes his own music.

Jack and Maria Farmer both work at the Arizona State University in Tempe. She is a faculty member and webmaster in the geography department, and he teaches geology and continues his research for NASA. They eat lunch together almost every day.

Jack Farmer enjoys studying rocks from Earth and Mars

The Martian meteorite ALH84001

perhaps a primitive form of bacterialike life. This was stunning news. If they were right, ALH84001 could contain the first evidence of life elsewhere in the Universe.

How do scientists know ALH84001 came from Mars? Gas trapped inside the meteorite is extremely similar to the Martian atmosphere.

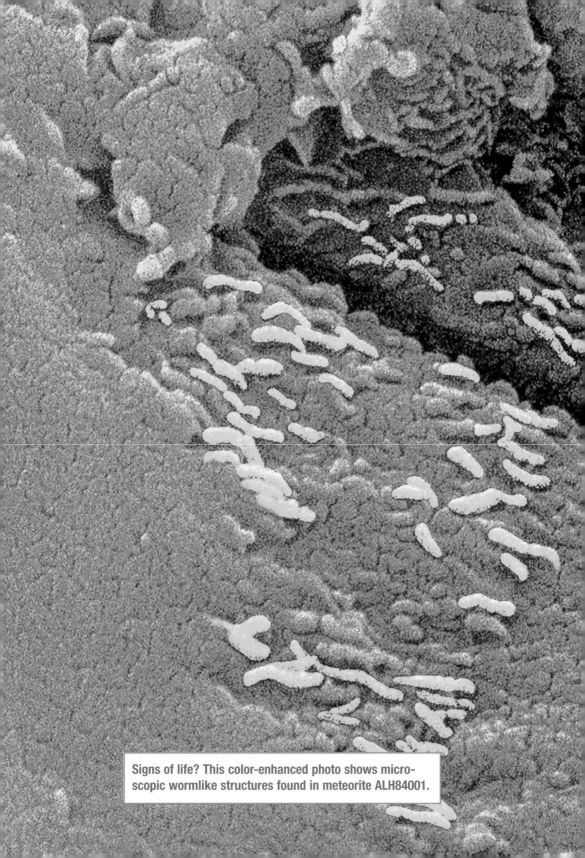

Signs of life? This color-enhanced photo shows microscopic wormlike structures found in meteorite ALH84001.

ALH84001 is not the only Martian meteorite scientists have encountered; at least a dozen others came from the red planet. Of course, none of these meteorites, including ALH84001, made a direct trip from Mars to Earth. After some catastrophic impact sent the chunk of rock flying into space, it traveled billions of years and huge distances to finally arrive here after orbiting many times around the solar system, approaching closer and closer, until it was finally caught by Earth's gravity. Then it plunged through our planet's atmosphere to the surface.

We know that meteorite ALH84001 is a 4.5-billion-year-old rock, and the fossil-like features it contains date back more than 3.6 billion years. It was dislodged from Mars some 16 million years ago and has been careening through space ever since, finally landing in the Antarctic 13,000 years ago. The meteorite's long journey ended at NASA's Johnson Space Center in Houston, Texas, where it now resides.

Many scientists question the conclusions made by the original group of investigators. Seen in greatly magnified images, the tiny tubular structures and other clues found in the rock do resemble some fossils found on our own planet. However, these tubular structures are ten times smaller than the tiniest bacteria on Earth. By the end of 1998, most experts agreed that the structures in the meteorite were not convincing evidence of past life on Mars. So the question we have been asking for hundreds of years remains unanswered.

Chapter 6

Future Missions to Mars

More than ever, scientists want to find answers to their questions about the red planet. Over the next few years, we will send a series of missions to do some serious exploring. The spacecraft will survey Mars's surface, collect samples of the atmosphere, search for signs of past and present life, and collect rocks and return them to Earth. A group of astronauts may even travel to Mars one day.

Back to Mars: The 10-Year Plan

NASA is serious about Mars, and the U.S. space organization is not alone. Japan, Great Britain, Russia, and France have also made commitments to explore the red planet. Beginning with the *Mars Pathfinder* and *Mars Global Surveyor* missions launched in 1996, NASA initiated a plan that called for sending two spacecraft to Mars

Mars Polar Lander was designed to help scientists learn more about climate change and current resources on Mars.

every 26 months for 10 years. It was an ambitious plan, and it would have undoubtedly provided us with some exciting results.

Each mission launched an orbiter, followed by a lander or a lander-rover combination like *Pathfinder* and *Sojourner*. The next pair, known as Mars Surveyor '98 (*Mars Climate Orbiter* and *Mars Polar Lander*), were scheduled to arrive in 1999. Unfortunately, *Mars Climate Orbiter* was lost as it entered orbit and *Mars Polar Lander* lost communication with Earth after descending toward the Martian surface. As a result, NASA began restructuring the plan, but future missions will probably be planned to combine or alternate orbiting spacecraft and landers.

These missions will look at Mars in several ways: as a planet, as a possible landing site for a human expedition, and as a comparison to Earth's atmosphere, geology, and history. They will:

- study the composition and seasonal changes of the Martian atmo-sphere.

- collect soil and rock samples to study Mars's surface chemistry and mineralogy. Some samples will be examined on the spot, using a tool kit or a preplanned set of experiments. Others will be sent back to Earth.

- look at the *topology*, or lay of the land.

- search for water on and below the surface.

Scientists hope this series of missions may settle questions about the past or present life on Mars. However, if they do not find signs of life, that will not prove that life never existed on Mars.

Mary Urquhart is a planetary scientist, but she is also a sort of computer modeling guru at NASA's Jet Propulsion Laboratory in Pasadena, California. Urquhart uses computers to study the atmospheres and surfaces of other planets. She has also studied three of Jupiter's moons and Earth's Moon.

In July 1999, Urquhart developed computer models to help prepare for the landing of the Deep Space 2/Mars Microprobe Mission. Her models tried to answer such questions as "What is the surface like at the landing site?" and "What will the temperature measurements mean, exactly?"

Urquhart uses computer models to mimic some of the important processes in nature. Because nature is far too complicated to use a computer to model all its processes at once, she has to decide which specific processes are most important to the problem she is looking at.

By the time Urquhart was in ninth grade, she knew that she wanted to be a planetary scientist. School had never been easy for her, though. She had a learning disability that made learning to read difficult. When she was young, she also had trouble with arithmetic—the numbers kept getting mixed up in her mind.

"In time, school became much easier," she says. "When I did learn to read, I read everything I could." She especially enjoyed reading science fiction, fantasy, and science books. It took a lot of effort, but she succeeded. Urquhart also developed interests in music and art, which made school more fun, she says. By the time she was in high school, she was on the honor roll.

"I learned at a very young age that curiosity is a good thing and that science is a life-long process of learning," Urquhart says. Scientists are always trying to find out more about how things work. "The best part of my job is that I get paid to learn, and sometimes I learn something that no one before me has ever known," adds Urquhart. "Science isn't all in books. It's about discovering new things and looking at the world in new ways. For me, it's also sharing that experience with others."

Mary Urquhart sits at her desk at NASA's Jet Propulsion Laboratory in Pasadena, California.

Destination Mars: A Human Voyage

Ever since the Apollo missions to the Moon, and for as long as cosmonauts have lived aboard the Russian space station *Mir* and astronauts have traveled and worked aboard the Space Shuttle, space visionaries and planners all over the world have been talking about a manned mission to the red planet. Never has it been such a real possibility as it is today.

Scientists predict that they may have the technology to accomplish this as soon as 2014. The international space station, which is currently being designed, could serve as a staging base for such a mission. A journey to Mars will be expensive—probably $20 billion or more—and the trip will be dangerous. We have never sent anyone so far from Earth. Many serious, even fatal, problems could arise. But people are already lining up eagerly for the job.

All NASA's current projects can help pave the way to Mars. An ion-propulsion engine aboard a little spacecraft called *Deep Space 1* (DS-1) sputtered to life in the fall of 1998. Like something out of a *Star Trek* episode, this engine uses power generated by shooting atomic particles out the back to propel a spacecraft forward. The spacecraft travels a little slower than those powered by traditional chemical rockets, but it's much cheaper to operate.

The *Mars Surveyor '01* orbiter is scheduled to launch in 2001 and arrive at Mars in 2002. The equipment onboard the orbiter will study the surface composition of the red planet and look for a variety of geological features, including dry lake beds and hydrothermal vents.

Future robot-lander missions will test methods for using a robot to extract methane fuel, oxygen, and water from the Martian soil and atmosphere. If these missions go well, NASA plans to use these

Mars Surveyor '01 will orbit Mars, as shown in this drawing. It will study the surface composition and look for both past and presently active areas (such as dry lakebeds and hydrothermal vents).

techniques to provide future astronauts with enough fuel for their return flight. The spacecraft that would carry them home would arrive on Mars and begin fueling up before the crew's outbound spaceship ever left Earth.

An inflatable three-story house called Transhab is also being tested at NASA's Johnson Space Center in Texas. Like a giant balloon made of material so tough it's bullet-proof, this house can collapse to a small size, fold up, and fit into a Space Shuttle cargo bay. Blown up to full size, it can serve as ample housing for astronauts living on Mars.

More Missions to Mars

Vital Statistics

Spacecraft	Type	Date of Launch*	Planned Date of Arrival	Sponsor
PLANET B/ NOZOMI (HOPE)	Orbiter	July 4, 1998	2004	Japan
MARS SURVEYOR '01 ORBITER	Orbiter	2001	2001	U.S.
MARS SURVEYOR '03 ORBITER	Orbiter	2003	2003	U.S.
MARS SURVEYOR '03 LANDER AND ROVER	Lander and rover	2003	2003	U.S.
MARS EXPRESS/ BEAGLE 2	Orbiter and lander	2003	2003	European Space Agency (ESA)/ United Kingdom
FRANCE/U.S. SURVEYOR '01 ORBITER	Orbiter, lander and robot	2005	2006	France and U.S.
SAMPLE RETURN MISSION	Orbiter	2005	2008	France

* More missions and micromissions are under consideration but still tentative.

In all, the crew would be away from Earth for about 2.5 years. The astronauts would spend 6 months traveling to Mars, about 1 year and 4 months exploring it, and 6 months returning to Earth. The six crew members would explore the geological formations and search for signs of life and clues about the origins of the solar system. This would be the Lewis and Clark Expedition of the twenty-first century.

Like Lewis and Clark, the astronaut pioneers would face many unknown dangers. They would also have the thrill of being the first humans ever to step on another planet. They would be the first people to experience the windstorms of Mars, watch the dunes drift across the rocky plains, and scale the sloping sides of Olympus Mons. They would be the first Earthlings to see this completely different world firsthand. What an exciting adventure that would be!

Vital Statistics

Spacecraft	Type	Date of Launch	Date of Arrival at Mars	Sponsor
MARS 1960A	Probable flyby	October 10, 1960	Failed	USSR
MARS 1960B	Probable flyby	October 14, 1960	Failed	USSR
MARS 1962A	Probable flyby	October 24, 1962	Failed	USSR
MARS 1	Flyby	November 1, 1962	Failed	USSR
MARS 1962B	Probable flyby	November 4, 1962	Failed	USSR
MARINER 3	Flyby	November 5 1964	Failed	U.S.
MARINER 4	Flyby	November 28, 1964	July 14, 1965	U.S.
ZOND 2	Flyby	November 30, 1964	Failed	USSR
MARS LANDER	Lander	March 27, 1967	Failed	USSR
MARINER 6	Flyby	February 24, 1969	July 31, 1969	U.S.

Spacecraft	Type	Date of Launch	Date of Arrival at Mars	Sponsor
MARINER 7	Flyby	March 27, 1969	August 5, 1969	U.S.
MARINER 8	Orbiter	May 8, 1971	Failed	U.S.
COSMOS 419	Orbiter/ lander	May 10, 1971	Failed	USSR
MARS 2	Orbiter/ lander	May 19, 1971	November 27, 1971	USSR
MARS 3	Orbiter/ lander	May 28, 1971	December 2, 1971	USSR
MARINER 9	Orbiter	May 30, 1971	November 13, 1971	U.S.
MARS 4	Orbiter	July 21, 1973	Failed	USSR
MARS 5	Orbiter	July 25, 1973	February 2, 1974	USSR
MARS 6	Orbiter/ lander	August 5, 1973	March 12, 1974	USSR
MARS 7	Orbiter/ lander	August 9, 1973	Failed	USSR
VIKING 1	Orbiter/ lander	August 20, 1975	July 19, 1976 (Mars orbit): July 20 (lander sets down on the surface)	U.S.
VIKING 2	Orbiter/ lander	September 9, 1975	September 3, 1976	U.S.
PHOBOS 1	Mars/ Phobos orbiter/ lander	July 7, 1988	Failed	USSR

Spacecraft	Type	Date of Launch	Date of Arrival at Mars	Sponsor
PHOBOS 2	Mars/Phobos orbiter/lander	July 12, 1988	January 30, 1989	USSR
MARS OBSERVER	Orbiter	September 25, 1992	Failed	U.S.
MARS GLOBAL SURVEYOR	Orbiter	November 7, 1996	September 12, 1997	U.S.
MARS-96	Orbiter/lander/probes	November 17, 1996	Failed	USSR
MARS PATHFINDER	Orbiter/lander/rover	December 4, 1996	July 4, 1997	U.S.
PLANET B/NOZOMI (HOPE)	Orbiter	July 4, 1998	Projected 2003	Japan
MARS SURVEYOR 98 (Mars Climate Orbiter, Mars Polar Lander, Deep Space 2 microprobes)	Orbiter/lander/probe	December 11, 1998 (orbiter) January 3, 1999	Failed	U.S.

Exploring Mars: A Timeline

1500s — Tycho Brahe (1546–1601) makes very accurate measurements of the orbit of Mars.

1543 — Publication of *On the Revolution of the Heavenly Spheres* by Nicolaus Copernicus (1473–1543). The book contains the revolutionary idea that all the planets (including Earth) orbit the Sun, challenging the widely accepted theory that Earth is at the center of the Universe.

1600 — Johannes Kepler begins to work with Tycho Brahe.

1610 — Italian physicist and astronomer Galileo Galilei observes Mars through a telescope.

1659 — Dutch physicist and astronomer Christiaan Huygens draws the first astronomical sketches of Mars.

1666 — The polar ice caps of Mars are discovered by Italian astronomer Giovanni Domenico Cassini.

1700s — English astronomer William Herschel finds the axial inclination of Mars.

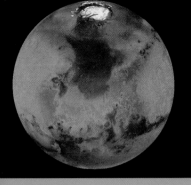

1877	G.V. Schiaparelli, an Italian astronomer, charts what he calls "canali" on the surface of Mars.
	Asaph Hall, an American astronomer, discovers the moons of Mars.
1895	Percival Lowell interprets Schiaparelli's "canali" as elaborate irrigation systems built by Martians.
1964	Ground-based observations detect water vapor on Mars.
1965	*Mariner 4* spacecraft shows Mars has a barren, cratered surface and no canals. The spacecraft also detects a thin atmosphere composed mostly of carbon dioxide.
1971	*Mars 3*, launched by the USSR, makes the first soft landing on Mars.
	Mariner 9 becomes the first Mars-orbiting spacecraft and makes the first map of Mars.
1976	*Viking 1* and *Viking 2* reach Mars. Their landers examine soil samples and test for signs of life.

1997 — The *Mars Pathfinder* lander arrives carrying *Sojourner*, a rover that explores the surface of Mars.

Mars Global Surveyor arrives in Mars orbit and begins taking images, including details of the north polar water ice cap.

1999 — *Mars Climate Orbiter* lost due to a navigational error. *Mars Polar Lander* also lost in December.

aerobraking—a method of slowing a spacecraft and lowering its orbit by using the force of friction between the spacecraft and a planet's atmosphere

asteroid—a piece of rocky debris left over from the formation of the solar system 4.6 billion years ago. Most asteroids orbit the Sun in a belt between Mars and Jupiter.

atmosphere—the gases that surround a planet or other body in space

axis—the imaginary line running from pole to pole through the center of a planet or moon. The celestial body spins, or rotates, along its axis.

comet—a small ball of rock and ice that travels toward the Sun in a long orbit that originates on the remote outer edge of the solar system

core—the innermost region of a moon or planet

crater—an irregular circular or oval depression in the surface of a planet or moon made by a collision with another object

crust—the outer surface of a moon or planet

diameter—the distance across the center of a circle or sphere

differentiation—the process of layering that takes place when the interior of a body melts, causing denser materials to sink to the center and lighter materials to rise to the surface. This process usually forms a core, mantle, and crust in the terrestrial planets.

elliptical orbit—an orbit that looks more like a flattened oval than a perfect circle

ellipse—a flattened oval

exobiologist—a biologist who studies the origins of life, early evolution, and the possibility of existence of life elsewhere in the solar system and the universe

fusion—a process in which enormous amounts of energy are released when certain chemical elements combine

gas giant—a very large planet composed mostly of gas. The four gas giants are Jupiter, Saturn, Uranus, and Neptune.

gravity—the force that pulls objects toward the center of a planet.

greenhouse effect—a natural warming process that occurs when the Sun's radiation reflected by a planet's surface is absorbed by carbon dioxide in the atmosphere and remains trapped on the planet; when carbon dioxide in an atmosphere reaches high levels

heresy—beliefs that are not in line with the opinions of those in power; in this case, the Roman Catholic Church

mantle—the region below the crust and above the core of a moon or planet

mass—the amount of matter or material in an object

meteorite—a particle of dust or rock that hits a moon or planet

meteoroid—a rocky or metallic object of relatively small size, usually once part of a comet or asteroid

planetesimal—precursor of a planet

shield volcano—a broad, rounded volcano

tectonic plate—one of several large pieces of a planet's crust. Earth has six major tectonic plates and about a dozen smaller ones. When these plates push against each other, mountain chains, rifts, and mid-ocean ridges form.

terrestrial planet—a rocky planet with a solid surface. Examples include Mars, Earth, Venus, and Mercury.

topology—a survey of the surface features of a geographic area.

The news from space changes fast, so it's always a good idea to check the copyright date on books, CD-ROMs, and videotapes to make sure that you are getting up-to-date information. One good place to look for current informtion from NASA is U.S. government depository libraries. There are several in each state.

Books

Bortz, Fred, and Alfred B. Bortz. *Martian Fossils on Earth? The Story of Meteorite ALH84001.* Brookfield, CT: Millbrook Press, 1997.

Campbell, Ann Jeanette. *Amazing Space: A Book of Answers for Kids.* New York: John Wiley & Sons, 1997.

Dickinson, Terence. *Other Worlds: A Beginner's Guide to Planets and Moons.* Willowdale, Ontario: Firefly Books, 1995.

Gustafson, John. *Planets, Moons and Meteors.* (The Young Stargazer's Guide to the Galaxy) New York: Julian Messner, 1992.

Hartmann, William K. and Don Miller. *The Grand Tour.* New York: Workman Publishing, 1993.

Schraff, Anne E. *Are We Moving to Mars?* Emeryville, CA: John Muir Publications, 1996.

Spangenburg, Ray, and Diane Moser. *Exploring the Reaches of the Solar System.* (Space Exploration) New York: Facts On File, Inc., 1990.

Vogt, Gregory L. *The Solar System Facts and Exploration.* Scientific American Sourcebooks. New York: Twenty-First Century Books, 1995.

Wunsch, Susi Trautmann. *The Adventures of Sojourner: The Mission to Mars That Thrilled the World.* New York: Mikaya Press, 1998.

CD-ROMs

Beyond Planet Earth. Discovery Channel School Multimedia, P.O. Box 970, Oxon Hill, MD 20750-0970.
An interactive journey to Mars and beyond. Includes video from NASA and Voyager missions and more than 200 photographs.

Organizations and Online Sites

Many of the online sites listed below are NASA sites, with links to many other interesting sources of information about moons and planetary systems. You can also sign up to receive NASA news on many subjects via e-mail.

Astronomical Society of the Pacific
http://www.aspsky.org/
390 Ashton Avenue
San Francisco, CA 94112

The Astronomy Café

http://www2.ari.net/home/odenwald/cafe.html

This site answers questions and offers news and articles related to astronomy and space. It is maintained by NASA scientist Sten Odenwald.

The Mars Society

http://www.marssociety.org

This group's goal is "the settlement and exploration of the red planet." You'll find links to many other sites of interest to Mars enthusiasts.

NASA Ask a Space Scientist

http://image.gsfc.nasa.gov/poetry/ask/askmag.html#list

Take a look at the Interactive Page where NASA scientists answer your questions about astronomy, space, and space missions. This site also has access to archives and fact sheets.

NASA Newsroom

http://www.nasa.gov/newsinfo/newsroom.html

This site features NASA's latest press releases, status reports, and fact sheets. It includes a news archive with past reports and a search button for the NASA website. You can even sign up for e-mail versions of all NASA press releases.

National Space Society
http://www.nss.org
600 Pennsylvania Avenue, S.E., Suite 201
Washington, DC 20003

The Nine Planets: A Multimedia Tour of the Solar System
http://www.seds.org/billa/tnp/nineplanets.html
This site has excellent material on the planets, including Mars. It was created and is maintained by the Students for the Exploration and Development of Space, University of Arizona.

Planetary Missions
http://nssdc.gsfc.nasa.gov/planetary/projects.html
At this site, you'll find NASA links to current and past missions. It's a one-stop shopping center for a wealth of information.

The Planetary Society
http://www.planetary.org/
65 North Catalina Avenue
Pasadena, CA 91106-2301

Mars Education Program (NASA/JPL)
http://marsnt3.jpl.nasa.gov/education/index-education.html
Designed for both students and teachers, this site provides a one-stop source for learning about Mars and missions to Mars.

Sky Online

http://www.skypub.com

This is the website for *Sky and Telescope* magazine and other publications of Sky Publishing Corporation. You'll find a good weekly news section on general space and astronomy news. Of special interest are *Sky and Telescope* feature stories adapted especially for online reading. The site also has tips for amateur astronomers as well as a nice selection of links. A list of science museums, planetariums, and astronomy clubs organized by state can help you locate nearby places to visit.

Welcome to the Planets

http://jpl.nasa.gov/planets/

This tour of the solar system has lots of pictures and information. The site was created and is maintained by California Institute of Technology for NASA/Jet Propulsion Laboratory.

Windows to the Universe

http://windows.ivv.nasa.gov/

This NASA site, developed by the University of Michigan, includes sections on "Our Planet," "Our Solar System," "Space Missions," and "Kids' Space." Choose from presentation levels of beginner, intermediate, or advanced. To begin exploring, go to the URL and choose "Enter the Site."

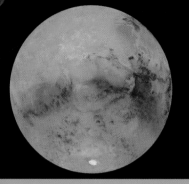

Places to Visit

Check the Internet (*www.skypub.com* is a good place to start), your local visitor's center, or phone directory for planetariums and science museums near you. Here are a few suggestions.

Exploratorium

3601 Lyon Street
San Francisco, CA 94123
http://www.exploratorium.edu/
You'll find internationally acclaimed interactive science exhibits, including astronomy subjects.

Jet Propulsion Laboratory (JPL)

4800 Oak Grove Drive
Pasadena, CA 91109
http://www.jpl.nasa.gov/faq/tours
JPL is the primary mission center for all NASA planetary missions. Tours are available once or twice a week by arrangement.

NASA Goddard Space Flight Center

Code 130, Public Affairs Office
Greenbelt, MD 20771
http://pao.gsfc.nasa.gov/
Visitors can see a Moon rock brought back to Earth by Apollo astronauts as well as other related exhibits.

National Air and Space Museum
7th and Independence Ave., S.W.
Washington, DC 20560
http://www.nasm.edu/nasm
This museum, located on the National Mall west of the Capitol building, has all kinds of interesting exhibits.

Space Center Houston
Space Center Houston Information
1601 NASA Road 1
Houston, Texas 77058
http://www.spacecenter.org/
Space Center Houston offers a tour and exhibits related to humans in space, including the Apollo missions to the Moon.

Bold numbers indicate illustrations.

Ray Spangenburg and **Kit Moser** are a husband-and-wife writing team specializing in science and technology. They have written 33 books and more than 100 articles, including a 5-book series on the history of science and a four-book series on the history of space exploration. As journalists, they covered NASA and related science activities for many years. They have flown on NASA's Kuiper Airborne Observatory, covered stories at the Deep Space Network in the Mojave Desert, and experienced zero-gravity on experimental NASA flights out of NASA Ames Research Center. They live in Carmichael, California, with their two dogs, Mencken (a Sharpei mix) and F. Scott Fitz (a Boston Terrier).